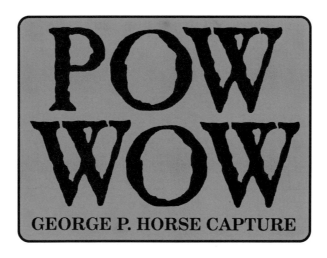

POW WOW

GEORGE P. HORSE CAPTURE

BUFFALO BILL
HISTORICAL
CENTER

**Many thanks to the Ford Foundation for helping
me along the Powwow Trail many years ago.**

PREFACE

The Buffalo Bill Historical Center has, since its inception over seventy years ago, been dedicated to preserving cultural traditions unique among western peoples. This mandate has led us to focus over the years as vigorously on centuries-old indigenous Indian forms of expression as on Anglo customs brought west by more recent arrivals.

This vision of cultural preservation was initially provided not by museum practitioners but by artists like George Catlin and by western exponents like William F. Cody. Their mutual cause was to preserve frontier customs and foster appreciation for their inherent beauty and integrity. Through that preservation and appreciation they also caused, in some instances, perpetuation of cultural form and element. Catlin's Indian dancers, presented throughout Europe in the mid-nineteenth century as *tableaux-vivants*, and Cody's recreated segments of Indian life and ritual enacted before enthusiastic late-nineteenth-century throngs in his Wild West arena, merged theatre with didacticism. Enjoyment was blended with instruction that informed both the audience and the participants.

Today's powwows serve a similar function. In revitalizing, reinforcing, preserving and promoting traditional patterns of Indian life, powwows provide continuity for generations of Indian people and a forum for enjoyment and learning for non-Indian observers. Here are opportunities to reveal enduring as well as innovative elements of dance, music, costume and social interplay among today's native celebrants.

For the past seven years the Buffalo Bill Historical Center has sponsored an annual powwow in Cody. Since 1987 that event has been hosted at the museum's Joe Robbie Powwow Garden. Therefore, it was appropriate, when Plains Indian Museum curator George Horse Capture suggested an exhibition and careful documentation of the modern Northern Plains powwow phenomenon, that the Historical Center step fully behind this interest and support it wholeheartedly. For here was a chance to fulfill our mission as an institution responsive to instruction and preservation.

Our thanks for this opportunity must first go to George, whose many years of participation and study of powwows engendered an interest in this project. We are indebted to the Dewey Dominick Fund for financial underwriting and to our staff members Robert Weiglein, Kay-Karol Horse Capture, Melissa Webster, and Joanne Kudla for their significant contributions to its success. Special thanks go to the many lenders of outfits which compose the exhibition, particularly to Al Chandler of Billings and Joe Day of Wolf Point, Montana; and to specific contributors such as the photographer Elijah Cobb of New York, Buffalo Chips of Cody, Sioux Trading Post of Rapid City, Western Trading Post of Denver, and June and Arne Sandberg of Cody.

Peter H. Hassrick
Director
Buffalo Bill Historical Center
Cody, Wyoming

INTRODUCTION

Accompanying major museum exhibitions, the catalog adds in-depth information, usually citing historical references that enhance one's interpretation of the subject to provide a unique perspective on the topic. This standard scholarly approach presented difficulties early on as we conceived this exhibit and began to make plans.

Said to be a Narragansett word meaning "medicine man," the contemporary usage of "powwow" refers to a living celebration of the Indian people of today and these events will continue with all their vigor, tradition, and change year after year, as long as there are Indian people in the world. Because of the importance of this topic, the catalog had to be special.

I decided that to document this continuing story with footnotes, citing references from early anthropological works, would rob it of its breathing vitality and relegate it, in some way, to the past. Instead, this "catalog," because of the nature of its topic, would take the form of a first-person narrative, a journal that presents an insider's view of this special activity; and I am grateful for all the assistance provided me by all my friends and fellow powwowers across Indian country. Think of how enlightening it would be if only we had such intimate first-person accounts of most of our key cultural and historical events. We could meet Lewis and Clark and Maximilian, listen to the great Indian chiefs, participate in battles, and all the rest; how much more we would know and understand.

This decision is not difficult once one realizes that the Buffalo Bill Historical Center is in the west. Located in Wyoming, our institution is literally surrounded by Indian tribes. The Arapaho and Shoshone people are but a few hours to the south, while another branch of the Shoshone and the Bannocks reside in Idaho, just west of Teton National Park. To the north in Montana are the Crow and Northern Cheyenne, and further north are the Blackfeet, Flathead, Chippewa, Cree, Assiniboine, Gros Ventre (my people) and the Sioux. Eastward lie the Dakotas and all of their tribes. The tribes and our museum are well aware of each other, and this interaction makes the Buffalo Bill Historical Center more responsive to these peoples. Our exhibits and programs are more reflective of this association.

In addition to the yearly celebration in our own Joe Robbie Powwow garden, usually the weekend before the Fourth of July, I attend and actively participate in many of the powwows and ceremonies on reservations in the west. This participation provides me with the perspective and knowledge necessary to present this exhibit, with its intimate view of what is happening in Indian country today.

The catalog focuses on the country and people I know and what they mean to me. No one publication can ever tell the complete story of a powwow, and these glimpses of my perceptions are but vignettes of what it is to be an Indian and to participate in powwows. To obtain the total picture and emotion one must attend an actual powwow. You will be welcome there. Come and visit Indian country.

So, if you expected a traditional catalog, you are in for a treat. Read, see, understand, and enjoy.

George P. Horse Capture
Curator
Plains Indian Museum
Buffalo Bill Historical Center
Cody, Wyoming

Women's Fancy Dancer. Owner: Oriann Baker, Chippewa, Sisseton Indian Reservation, South Dakota.

Princess. Owner: Kaylene Shane, Crow, Crow Indian Reservation, Montana.

The Setting

It is springtime at last, and the highway stretches out before us without a curve as we speed along in our loaded van. The prairie on Chapman Bench, north of Cody, Wyoming, is gently greening, though the dividing line between winter and springtime is not as dramatic and colorful as usual because of the warm, dry winter. A few rainstorms accompanied·the arrival of spring, and the prairie is lovely as it comes alive once again. With the beauty of spring comes the beauty of tradition. After many months of anticipation we are all packed, loaded with our dance outfits and folding chairs, and are heading north on Highway 120 to the Red Bottom Celebration to powwow.

The tensions of the week are easing as we hum along, and the kids are quieting down in the back seats, reading and finding other things to occupy the many hours ahead. The hustle and the hassle of packing are all but forgotten as we each, in our own way, look forward to seeing friends and relatives and to experiencing all the other things that happen in the springtime in our country.

Newscasters warn that there is a drought coming. For now, birds are singing and all the valley and coulee bottoms are lush with greenery and the trees are brilliantly shaggy with their new plumage. Only a few ice fields remain on the upper reaches of the mountains, and maybe the forecasters are right. But for now, the beauty of the countryside is overwhelming.

The Country

This region is very special because of its components. About ten miles to the west, the Absaroka mountain range, named for the Crow Indian people, rises up in spectacular grandeur. The Absarokas are part of a larger mountain chain called the Cordillera which extends from northern Alaska all the way down the hemisphere, south to the tip of Tierra del Fuego, forming the spine of our continent.

Some theorists say that after entering North America tens of thousands of years ago, the first immigrants made their way to the eastern side of these mountains. Keeping them in sight to the west and moving south whenever the glaciers cleared, they eventually entered what is now called the United States; and many of these First Americans continued south, enjoying the harvest from the mountains and the plains.

To the east of Chapman Bench lie the plains. Far from being "the Great American Desert" as proclaimed by the early settlers, this area abounded in massive herds of buffalo, and the Indian people followed them for centuries. The buttes or points, the most prominent geological features of the plains, have circles or piles of stones on them, attesting to their early occupancy by Indian holy men. We will never know the full story of these early people, but they were thriving here scores of centuries ago.

Scholars say that after the ancient Indian people crossed the Bering Strait that connected Siberia to Alaska, the weather changed, causing the continental glaciers to melt and the seas to rise, eventually covering with water the entryway between the old and new worlds and isolating these first arrivals. With the other early people in the old world continuing to mix with one another, it would be many centuries before they would occupy general areas and bear specific racial terms or names. Isolated on a previously uninhabited hemisphere, the Indian people remained comparatively pure; there were no other groups with whom to mix. So, it can be said that the Indian people are the oldest identifiable race in the world. How about that?

This Northern Plains area is immense, and while driving along the valley bottoms, one can look around and experience the cleanliness of the air and the beauty of the landscape. Animals are everywhere.

Farmers now grow a wide variety of crops here. Sugar beets, hay, corn and many other cultivated crops color the plowed earth on either side of the road as we travel past. The commercials say that the Indian people call corn "maize." Did anyone ever correlate this term with a known native language? Everyone I know calls it "corn."

As children on the Fort Belknap Indian Reservation in northern Montana, we frequently went into the local white farmers' cornfields to play. When the leaves on the main stalk enlarge, the fields really are a maze. It was a great place to play hide and seek. When we got hungry, if the time of year was right, we could just reach up and pop off an ear, strip off the husk and silk and eat the kernels raw. Nothing is quite as sweet—with the

Camp housing.

exception of June berries, of course.

The miles of travel to powwows seem endless but never boring. Once in a while a squabble between the children flares up but soon subsides. We always have the option of listening to the radio when we are close to a town, but the radio signal dies out in the middle of the prairie, and our backup is always audio cassettes.

The Music

After a long winter in town doing all those city-type things, we know we have been engaged solely in non-Indian activities. So, as we travel we subtly reintroduce Indianness to our children. We start by playing Indian songs on the automobile cassette player. One of our favorites is by the Young Grey Horse Society singers from the Blackfeet.

Long ago, when my father was a young man, his generation and the previous one lived through some hard times. They were made to feel ashamed of their Indianness. It was during this period that, in order to protect the children, the Indian people tried to learn the white ways. As a result, many of our customs faded and our language was not passed on. In the 1960's, in the Indian Awareness Movement, my generation realized that it was good and special to be Indian. We began to search for the elements of our culture. Upon realizing the importance of our language and knowing many of us could never speak it, we were horrified,

Drum and drumsticks.

ashamed and saddened by its tragic loss.

Some Indian people accepted this situation as inevitable and moved into the white society as best they could. But many others enrolled in colleges to gain skills to work for and with their people. For the first time in our history, hundreds of Indian people became full-fledged college students. In addition to pursuing scholarly studies of their people, the students were well aware of their native oral tradition and knew that many key parts of the culture were passed on in this manner (as they still are to this day). We know that the early anthropologists and others recorded most of our origin stories and therefore know of Spider and Coyote. But one elusive cultural element they could not quite grasp is our music.

For those who lived off-reservation and participated only in occasional powwows, it was quite difficult to learn to sing Indian songs. They have few or no words, and to understand their structures and to memorize them is difficult to learn on one's own. There are virtually no books on the subject, but we had to try; Indian people cannot be mere cultural observers but must be active life-long participants. By listening to tapes and records over and over again, one can eventually begin to detect the structure. If one can divide the song into the proper segments and understand and feel the phrases and rhythms, one can learn a song thoroughly. Once one song is learned, the following ones become easier.

Young Girl's Jingle Dress Dancer. Owner: Myrtle Old Man, Arapaho, Arapahoe, Wyoming.

Girl's Tiny Tot Jingle Dress Dancer. Owner: Audrey Belgarde, Chippewa, Billings, Montana.

Music is a part of everyone's life. All groups of people in the world share the same basic traits that make humans different from the other animals. Among these higher developments is the love of dance and music. By living in different places, various groups develop cultural patterns and ways of life that satisfy their particular needs. Often we can recognize these special groups by their unique musical traditions.

An easily identifiable, but little understood, musical tradition is that of the American Indian. Although this music is centuries old, it is still being performed today with all of its natural vigor and it has maintained its ancient structure. This strength of culture keeps the first people of this continent closer together than most other groups in this country.

Few non-Indian people recognize the importance of song to the American Indian. Fewer still can detect the structure of our songs because they are vastly different from the European or "American" ones. To the untrained ear all Indian songs may sound alike. One can understand this situation better by comparing "hard rock" to "disco" sounds. To the untrained or unappreciative ear, they too sound alike; but their individuality is probably readily distinguished by connoisseurs of those styles. And so it is with Indian songs.

Our Plains Indian dance songs generally contain four major verses. (The sacred number four can be observed in many cultural traits of the Indian people). The verses are alike and each can be further subdivided into two groupings, and these can be divided into two like components.

The first two components of a verse are the same, as are the last two. Together these four elements form a verse, with four verses making up a song. By recognizing and memorizing the two different components, one can easily learn to sing that song. The songs are based on repetition and the number four. If this rule is remembered, understanding will be easier.

Each song is started by the lead singer, who begins alone with high sequential notes introducing the song. The second singer cuts into the introductory component before it is completed and the entire group takes up the song. The lead singer's voice ends and later blends in with the rest as the notes cascade downward to lower ones, finishing the verse or "push up".

Three-fourths of the way through the second verse of a regular song, heavily accented drum beats note a change in tempo and the pace quickens until the end of the song. Recently this acceleration has been occurring at the end of the lead singer's introduction of the third verse.

An understanding of a song's structure eases the way for a dedicated learner.

Indian songs have few words; most songs have none. Years ago only the Sioux people favored wording. Most tribal songs use vowel-like sounds such as "hey, yah, lay," which occur between the drum beats. The exact "vowels" are not as important as their tones or notes in the musical scale. In fact, like most others, Indian songs can be whistled or hummed. Each note has a specific place in relation to the other notes. This is very important because usually there are no easy words to remember; only the melodies are vital. Once a melody is remembered, the remainder of the song can be sung.

The Indian people of Canada have long been a repository and garden of Indian music. It is well known that when Indian traditions were undergoing attack in the "Lower 48," they were alive and well up north. Since then songs have been passed south into the Dakota states, then west into Montana and Wyoming, then out to the world.

The most recent rage to make this trek is a new style of singing. Said to have "originated" in Chiniki Lake in Alberta about three years ago, the new style uses Lakota or Nakota Indian words extensively, replacing much of the vowel-like sounds. I discussed this phenomenon with Chris Eagle Hawk, a Lakota member of the Crazy Horse Singers. He said that unlike the Sioux songs of long ago whose words told a story of honor or bravery, today's songs in this category tell no logical story, but like the Beach Boys, urge one to "dance, dance, dance."

These new style songs are gaining in popularity, and the novel method offers brisker, more controlled sounds that can be more easily memorized. The Chiniki Lake Singers may have reached the summit of recognition, with the Stoney Lake and Blackstone Singers not far behind. All are from Canada.

A boyhood friend, Gordon Lodge, a Gros Ventre member of the Hays Singers, remembers that as a boy when he and close friend

A drum singing group at the Rosebud.

Bobby Talks Different wanted to learn to sing, they sat in with a family group and for several years were only allowed to tap the rim of the drum while the group performed. This long apprenticeship was necessary so that they both had a lengthy exposure to singers, their songs and their subtle nuances.

Today, Gordon says, times have changed. Long ago, the singer's voice had to be high, clear and strong in order to carry to the far reaches of the community hall or powwow arbor. Now, amplifiers allow even the smallest sound to project everywhere. He says that today one can even whisper a song.

Other groups use parabolic clip-on microphones and floor-activated electronic voice enhancers. Although the old ways are changing, the innovations allow more and more drum groups to be effective, and that is always good.

Wherever there are Indian people, there is Indian music. Songs are not just for pleasure. They also serve many useful purposes. In the old days, it was said that songs came from supernatural sources. The social songs are of a later phase and are less important.

Songs have many purposes: for courting, marking social and religious events, curing the ill, and praying. There are songs for many other purposes, even for death.

Indian people have a unique musical system. There are no set rules of composition, no teachers and no concerts. Yet, like many aspects of our culture, the music has endured for many thousands of years.

Several years ago, after finally learning how to sing more than one song and feeling pretty confident, I made a proposition to my children: the two older boys, my daughter and her younger brother. After showing them the beauty of a warbonnet that a relative had just given to me as a gift, I explained the importance of owning such an item, and how it is a badge of honor. I explained that being a singer of Indian songs is very special and a key to helping us survive as a distinct and unique people. I went on to say that we lived most of the time in a white world where it is difficult to be exposed to these Indian cultural necessities. I asked them to make an extra effort to learn to sing Indian. Addressing them all equally, but talking primarily to the two older boys, I said whoever learned to sing an Indian song from

Getting ready for the Grand Entry.

beginning to end with no mistakes would be the owner of my only eagle feather warbonnet. I gave them a year. Time passed, and I would occasionally hear the encouraging sound of a far-off drum beating somewhere. About a year later my dreams were answered, because it was then, after a brief self-introduction, that I heard the first Indian song proudly sung by one of my children from beginning to end without a mistake. And, as promised, my daughter Daylight, the singer, now owns that warbonnet.

Now with the chain reestablished, the circle is repaired, and many in our family will once again be singers like they were long ago. Even now, after driving several hours, I will take down the drumstick tucked behind the sun visor and sing one of our favorites. One by one, the children and my non-Indian wife are caught up in the power of the song, and with varying intensities, join in. Even our granddaughter Elizabeth knows a Flathead Indian stick game song, and she is teaching it to her brother Sage who is not yet three years old.

Women's Traditional Dancer. Owner: Gloria Goggles, Sioux, Ethete, Wyoming.

Men's Traditional Dancer. Owner: George P. Horse Capture, Gros Ventre, Cody, Wyoming.

Traveling

We cross the Yellowstone River and soon hit Highway 90. After a few minutes traveling east we are in Billings, Montana's largest city, where we spend the night. The stop is a welcome one, for the kids' activity and energy level is rising against their cramped confinement.

In the morning we head east again through the valley of the Yellowstone River, which is one of the few major rivers in the United States still left unencumbered by the damn dams. The road and river weave eastward toward the Yellowstone's confluence with the Missouri River at Fort Union, frequently meeting and crossing each other along the way. The river is clear and beautiful, and like most in the West, it had an essential role in the early exploration of this country. For it is upon these moving highways that the first explorers entered Indian country.

Another attractive aspect about traveling here is that the country is heavily sprinkled with historic sites in various forms. Some we know and some, of course, we will never know. Soon we will be approaching Pompey's Pillar, adjacent to the Yellowstone. On his return trip to the Pacific Ocean, Captain Clark of the Lewis and Clark Expedition noticed this landmark. "Pillar" implies a tall, slim, uniform, round column rising skyward. But this feature is a prairie pillar, and made of dirt. Instead of being a uniform, shaft-like column, this is a mesa structure standing by itself, lower than the adjacent rimrocks. The grassy top is now adorned by an American flag with the circular cliff measuring approximately 100 feet high and 200 feet in diameter. On one of its cliffs one can enjoy seeing the name of "Wm. Clark," where he carved it on July 25, 1806.

A few miles south is the Crow Indian Reservation, and further east is the Northern Cheyenne Reservation. Of course, both of these colorful areas are loaded with historic sites. Our whole country is, and we become closer to its history and significance by traveling and actually seeing these things. It makes us one with the land.

We continue eastward on Montana Interstate 94 until we reach Miles City and then turn north on Highway 22 across the flat plains of eastern Montana. Even this country is beautiful.

Later we cross the Fort Peck Dam and enter Montana Highway

Three generations. Irene White & her family, Wood, South Dakota.

Dancing buddies at Robbie Powwow Garden, Buffalo Bill Historical Center, Cody, Wyoming.

2 at Nashua. Now we are only 15 minutes from Frazer, and we have just crossed the mighty Missouri and are about 50 miles from Canada.

This highway is called "the High Line," a route that extends across Montana near its northern reaches. It was first mapped by Governor Isaac I. Stevens in 1853-1855, when he made the survey for the Great Northern Railroad. The railroad tracks are still here as testimony.

The Camp

A little beyond Nashua is the western boundary of the Fort Peck Indian Reservation, home of the Assiniboine and Sioux Indian people. It extends eastward for about 80 miles. Its southern border is the Missouri River. We see the grain elevators by the railroad tracks rising in the south, and we know we have arrived at the Red Bottom Clan's Annual Indian Celebration.

The camp, adjacent to the highway, has no discernible layout from ground level, and is packed with campers, RVs, umbrella, dome, and wall tents, and tipis. It would not be surprising to see a condo or just a cave somewhere out there. It has been two years since we attended this celebration, so we drive around the camp to look things over.

An old Indian once said that there are three basic ingredients for a powwow. One, of course, is Indians. Two is that dust must be in the air everywhere, so fine that it will stop a waterproof watch. The third is that the old, ramshackle, broken-down outhouses must be filled to overflowing. The first two are still requirements. The third ingredient may be history. The new fiberglass molded toilets are contracted out; cleaned and washed down daily.

A custom of old that is rapidly fading is providing rations to the camp. This action is undoubtedly an extension of the custom of feeding a guest. Rations can take many forms, but usually the main staples are meat, bread, and a vegetable. These gifts are delivered by truck. Every "camp" qualifies, whether it be an RV, tipi or tent; and to feed a camp of 200 or 300 units is quite an obligation.

Most powwow committees today try to feed everyone at least once. Brown bag lunches or even buffalo barbecues can fulfill this obligation. Several times during the dancing, a family may sponsor a "give-away" feed and invite all singers and/or dancers and/or everyone to their "camp" or to the local gym to eat. Generosity is alive and well in powwow country, and no one goes hungry.

All powwow camps provide water. Unmonitored faucets are spread throughout the grounds, and it is here that the people can get drinking water or water for their coffee or Kool-Aid. It is also the wallow for playing and squirting children, as well as a growing source of mud for deerskin moccasins and automobiles.

A proper camp must have tipis. These beautiful structures are more than mere shelters. They are symbols of the Plains Indian people and must be presented proudly. The more attractive ones always have their covers stretched taut and nearly touching the ground on all sides; "high water" sides mark the inexperienced erector. For some stereotypical reasons, non-Indians seem to feel that all tipis should be painted. Painting a tipi is serious business. Only "qualified" people can undertake such a task, and the designs should be traditional and used only with permission of the owners. If these tenets are ignored, the designs are only cartoons.

The poles should be long and slim, extending beyond the apex almost as far as that portion covered by the canvas. This extended "excess" of poles can be compared to fringes on clothing. Neither serves a specific utilitarian purpose; their sole function is balance and beauty. The weight and bulk of poles at least 25 feet long present a dilemma for travelers. With a growing number of powwowers unable to carry poles and fewer and fewer powwows supplying them, the majority of tipis now belong to locals.

As we continue our "survey" we see my Uncle Roosevelt and know that my aunts and other uncles are camped in their usual position. We will visit them later. One section is reserved for the police, and we see a number of their cars on the alert. Adjacent to them is an ambulance, also pointed outward and manned. We choose a little corner area in which to park the van. Although it is adjacent to the road, the hazard is worthwhile because we have easy access for departure.

The grand entry has already started, and we are disappointed that we missed it. This is the most important event of all, but we

Grass Dancer. Owner: Jay Fox, Northern Cheyenne, Busby, Montana.

Girl's Fancy Dancer. Owner: Margret Ross, Mandan/Hidatsa, Garrison, North Dakota.

were not suited up anyway. Our disappointment is short-lived, and we enjoy the action. The dancers are in a flurry of activity. We find space in the crowded grandstand and look on. Home at last.

Every Indian community is sort of a mini-home. Although other Indian reservations are not our own, they are still Indian and that provides comfort. There is a general unifying relationship among all Indians, but being on your own reservation is special. During the powwow season we and several thousand other Indian people across the country travel many hundreds of miles as often as possible to participate in these celebrations and ceremonies usually held on Indian reservations.

Bob Four Star, a popular emcee, jokes that it gets so hot here that they were going to hire a rain maker. He says, "Yeah, they were going to hire a rain maker. They were going to get a white man from Wolf Point to come out here and wash his car."

I see a number of white people dancing, and they are doing very nicely. Nobody pays them any attention. As we sit, friends stop by and shake hands and visit awhile. It's good to see that we all made it through another year. I saw a friend here a few years ago, Dennis Granbois. I remembered he had a little girl and inquired as to her whereabouts. He said, "She's around here somewhere. She's now old enough to travel with the pack, so we don't see her much during the powwow."

The Clothing

A friend and superb bead worker from Ft. Hall, Sandra Ariwite, once told me, "Never call our powwow clothing 'costumes.' Clowns wear costumes; this is our real powwow dress."

Men

It would be too complex and lengthy to describe the attire of every category of the powwow dancer. Many items on the male dancer's assemblage can be found in all male categories, so a brief description of these "typical" items will provide a basic outline.

At the top of the body is the headdress. It is an attractive item made primarily of long porcupine guard hairs on the edge of the 20-inch teardrop-shaped base, trimmed with a shorter row of deer tail hair along the outside edge. The long hair emphasizes body movements. This piece is always called a headdress because it dresses up the head. Nowadays many people call it a roach, a term from the southern plains, probably because the trimmed look is similar to the upstanding hair of a horse's mane after it has been cropped. Roaches are difficult to construct and are very beautiful. One can compare them to the brush-topped Roman soldier's helmet.

Next are facial paints. Colors and patterns are selected because of their particular meaning to the wearer. One might paint one's face in the style of an ancestor, to carry on a family style or because of personal power. Nothing here is casual: symmetry, neatness and meaning are essential.

There is an old Indian saying that warns, "Never trust a person who must wear a choker to 'prove' that they are Indian." Pretenders often think that if they wear a choker, it will mean they are Indian. That observation does not hold at powwows, because real Indian men and women often wear chokers made of hairpipe or dentalium, or necklaces made of cloth or beads. Even colorful scarves decorate the neck.

Over the chest area there could also be a hairpipe breastplate or an otterskin decorated with small mirrors. A beadwork harness or loop necklace can also be worn in combination with other items. Even narrow hairpipe bandoleers are worn in this manner.

The torso may be covered with a calico cloth ribbon shirt or one that sparkles and shines. Some have no torso covering at all.

On the back of the shoulders and waist the fancy dancers wear brightly colored bustles of dyed chicken hackle feathers. Traditional dancers wear only black-tipped eagle feather wing bustles at the back of their waists. The elders limit their attire to warbonnets worn with buckskin vests and trousers.

Most dancers wear some type of armband of beadwork, quillwork, featherwork, animal skin strips and many other types of interesting materials.

Belts can be beaded, plain, paneled or woven. They are often made wide to cover up various ties and other belts underneath. Swimming trunks or other shorts are usually worn under the breechcloth which hugs the hips and hangs down as a panel in front.

Some of the men's legs are bare while others are encased in

"Make me proud."

leather or cloth leggings. Bells are usually worn at the mid-calf or ankle area for maximum sound impact or are strung down the middle of the outside of each leg or legging. Brass, large steel or sheep bells are the best, while the wrinkled, tinny jingle bells are unacceptable.

Near the ankle, below the bells, bands of long hair from Angora sheep are worn. Perhaps they mimic the fetlocks of the horse, but they visually accent the dancer's steps and provide balance. Strips of fringed leather instead of the expensive hair are sometimes used by dancers. Only beaded leather moccasins should be worn at powwows, although some tribes seem to prefer tennis shoes and athletic socks. I hope that this phase is fading.

Dancers may also wear beaded gloves or carry fans, whistles, pouches, mirror boards, coup sticks, shields, or wheels.

Women

The women's attire is just as attractive and dynamic as the males' and perhaps more creative.

The older ladies prefer their hair braided, while some of the youngsters let theirs hang free. A beaded disk or quilled "medicine" wheel may hold feathers and the hair. Fur skins are wrapped around the braids, dangling nearly to the ground. Lately, headbands as well as princess's crowns are worn. This is not a traditional style. Headbands appear only in early paintings which formed the stereotype of the Indian "maiden" or "princess." Spreading outward from the southern plains in recent times, headbands are now being incorporated into the culture.

Two basic types of dresses are always worn by female dancers – buckskin and cloth. One is made of deerskin decorated with beadwork or shells; the other is wool, satin, or other material decorated with ribbons, tin cones, or other items. Traditionally the chest area is decorated with a hairpipe breastplate. Chokers or scarves of various materials may be worn around the neck; and some women wear a long strand of beads, wrapped around many times. On the arms a shawl may be carried, as may fans, purses, or other bags. A colorful phenomenon is the yokes that at one time were attached to the top of the dresses but now, on the younger dancers, they are detachable and are often placed on top of the shawls or removed during the hotter part of the day.

Going for the Fancy Dance money. Photo: Sue Ostrowski, The Cody Enterprise.

Women's Jingle Dress Dancer. Owner: Danna Clark-Runs Above, Assiniboine, Ft. Peck Indian Reservation, Montana.

Women's Traditional Dancer. Owner: Emily Day, Sioux/Assiniboine, Ft. Peck Indian Reservation, Montana.

A belt may be made of plain leather or canvas decorated with conchos, brass tacks or beads. This colorful piece not only holds other items such as knife cases, awls, and pouches, but also divides the vertical appearance of the wearer, making the total picture much more attractive.

The buckskin dresses are long and the ribbonwork dresses are shorter. The cloth dresses can be worn with both beaded and cloth leggings, but only the beaded ones are proper with the buckskin dresses. Fringed leather is sometimes substituted for the regular ankle leggings just as it is in the leg decoration for the male dancers. Only leather footwear is traditionally acceptable.

The only requirement for females to dance is that they have a shawl. With a shawl over their shoulders, they can dance in their suits, or even Levis, although abbreviated clothing is frowned upon.

The men must be fully attired in traditional garb in order to dance. The exceptions to this rule are guests, singers who carry their drumsticks, and those who wear warbonnets. Joe Day, an Assiniboine/Sioux friend from the Ft. Peck Reservation, says that among his clan a man can dance in his "civilian" clothes as long as he wears an eagle feather in his hat.

The history and usage of materials and customs pertaining to Indian dances are very complex and dynamic. Over a period of time, new styles and materials are introduced, while others disappear. The essential customs that are maintained have their base in old ceremonies and will continue.

Feathers

Certain feathers are protected by federal law. The following is an excerpt from Feathers and Federal Law (U.S. Department of the Interior, FS-11, April, 1975):

What species of birds are protected by Federal law?

The Migratory Bird Treaty Act offers protection to all wild birds found commonly in the United States, except the house sparrow, starling, feral pigeon, and resident game birds such as pheasant, grouse, quail, wild turkeys, etc. Resident game birds are managed by the separate States, and may be taken and their feathers and parts utilized as prescribed by State law. A reference list of migratory birds can be found in Title 50, Code of Federal Regulations, Part 10. The Bald Eagle Protection Act affords additional protection to all bald and golden eagles. Additionally, some species of migratory birds are provided further protection by the Endangered Species Act of 1973.

What activities do these laws prohibit?

*The Migratory Bird Treaty Act makes it unlawful for anyone to kill, capture, collect, possess, buy, sell, trade, ship, import or export any migratory bird, **including feathers, parts, nests or eggs**, unless the person first obtains an appropriate Federal permit in compliance with Federal regulations on migratory birds (see 50 CFR Part 21). The Bald Eagle Protection Act likewise prohibits all commercial activities involving bald or golden eagles, including their feathers or parts.*

Some migratory game birds may be lawfully hunted during specified periods but may not be sold. Annually published Federal hunting regulations (50 CFR Part 20) impose limits on the number and kinds of birds that can be taken, and control the manner, means and open seasons within which such taking is lawful.

Why does the Federal government prohibit commercial traffic in the feathers and parts of eagles and migratory birds?

Because migratory birds cross international boundaries in many cases, they are considered an international resource that must be protected from commercial exploitation. The Migratory Bird Treaty Act, passed in 1918 and subsequently amended, implements treaties for the protection of migratory species signed with Great Britain (for Canada), Mexico and Japan. The Bald Eagle Protection Act was passed in 1940 to protect our national bird, which at the time was rapidly declining in numbers. The golden eagle was given protection under the Bald Eagle Protection Act in 1962. In 1972, an amendment to the treaty with Mexico also included eagles as migratory birds, and afforded these birds protection under the Migratory Bird Treaty Act.

As the popularity of American Indian artifacts has increased in recent years, a lucrative market has developed for the eagle and migratory bird feathers used to make or decorate many Indian curios and art objects. The result has been the slaughter of

Intense Traditional Dancing or "The Fate of Wiley Coyote".

thousands of birds to fill this demand for feathers, and other parts such as beaks, bones, and talons. The prohibitions against commercial traffic in eagles and migratory birds are intended to eliminate any market for the birds themselves, or for their feathers and parts.

Are there any legally recognized commercial uses of feathers or parts of protected birds?

As a general rule, feathers or parts of migratory birds or eagles may not be sold, traded or bartered or offered for sale. However, these items may be displayed (without price tags) in shops or at shows and powwows. In addition, any person may possess, purchase, sell, barter, or transport for the making of fishing flies, bed pillows and mattresses and for similar commercial uses, the feathers of migratory water fowl (wild ducks, geese, brant and swans) legally taken in accordance with 50 CFR Part 20.

Can an individual make items from the feathers of protected birds for his own personal use?

*Any person **for his own** use may possess, transport, and ship, without a permit, the feathers, parts and skins of **lawfully** taken migratory **game** birds. A permit is required for import or export. While feathers and parts of migratory **non-game birds**, bald eagles and golden eagles may not be possessed by any person without appropriate Federal permits unless the feathers or parts were acquired prior to the date when Federal protection was provided for individual species (see below), it is the current policy of the Department of the Interior not to take legal action against any American Indian who merely possesses migratory bird or eagle feathers. This is in recognition of the role that migratory bird feathers have in American Indian religious practice. We stress, however, that the Department is not authorizing commercial traffic in protected birds and their parts, even among Indians. As noted above, **all** persons are allowed to possess or transport, but not sell, feathers or parts of protected birds, if the birds, feathers or parts were lawfully obtained prior to the date the species in question was first protected by Federal law. The bald eagle has been protected since 1940; the golden eagle since1962. The first migratory birds were protected in 1918; however, numerous amendments to the Migratory Bird Treaty Act have since protected additional species. Please check with the Special*

Pair of Eagle feathers.

Women's Traditional Dancer. Owner: Dawn Chandler, Gros Ventre, Beaverton, Oregon.   Women's Jingle Dress Dancer. Owner: Denise Lajimodiere, Belcourt, North Dakota.

Agent in Charge of the U.S. Fish and Wildlife Service Law Enforcement District in your area, to find out when a particular species was first afforded protection.

Indians require the feathers of protected birds for use in their religious or cultural activities. How can they obtain feathers for these purposes?

American Indians may possess, carry, use, wear, give, loan or exchange among other Indians, but without compensation, all Federally protected birds, as well as their parts or feathers. American Indians who wish to possess bird feathers or parts to be worked on by tribal craftsmen for eventual use in Indian religious or cultural activities may transfer such feathers or parts to tribal craftsmen without charge, but such craftsmen may be compensated for their work.

In addition, American Indians can obtain feathers and parts of bald or golden eagles for use in bona fide religious ceremonies. Free permits for distribution of eagle feathers for religious purposes are available from the U.S. Fish and Wildlife Service. The Service salvages the remains of eagles killed in the wild, or which die naturally in zoos, for distribution to Indians for religious purposes from a newly established repository in Pocatello, Idaho. Eagle feathers, however, are not obtainable from this source for sale or other commercial activities.

Information on how to apply for eagle feather permits can be obtained by writing to the Special Agent in Charge of the Fish and Wildlife Service Law Enforcement District serving your area.

Indian people can obtain eagle feathers by contacting their regional office of the U.S. Fish and Wildlife Service. By asking for a Permit Application Form #3-200, they will be sent a packet that contains, among other things, a form that must be signed by a Bureau of Indian Affairs official confirming their Indian blood and tribal membership. Another part of this form must be signed by a tribal official stating that these feathers will be used for religious purposes.

When approved by the regional office, the federal repository in Ashland, Oregon, will send the applicant all or parts of an eagle. The feathers are usually the worse for wear.

Most Indian people believe that eagle feathers are very special and are from the majestic bird that carries our prayers to The

Traditional dancers with Michael Ziegler, Brule Sioux, in foreground.

One Above. By wearing these attractive items we hope to gain some of the beauty, strength, dignity and spirituality they possess. It has always been so. Any type of commercialism of these sacred objects desecrates this age-old belief.

New Styles

Watching the incredible diversity of dancing attire during the first dance contest confirms several observations. The hottest new items on the Plains Powwow circuit are the yarn-fringed "Grass Dance" suits and the tin-coned Jingle dresses. The Jingle dresses are form-fitting, brightly colored dresses with tin cones attached. There is a profusion of them here, more so than in many parts of South Dakota, even though this site is farther from their point of origin. They are quite striking and add colorful sounds to the women. There is even a Jingle dress here made of buckskin — incredible.

Jingle dresses have an interesting history. Perhaps twenty years ago while working in the local Indian friendship house in the San Francisco Bay area, I first noticed this type of dress. The following original story of the dress was provided by Denise Lajimodiere, a Chippewa Jingle dress dancer from Belcourt, North Dakota.

"In a dream, a special dress and dance appeared to a holy man on the Mille Lacs Reservation, Minnesota. In his dream four women appeared wearing these dresses. They showed him how to make them and the songs that went with them. The dresses were different. They had metal cones on them that made a pretty sound.

"After awakening, the holy man and his wife made the special dresses and had four women present them at a dance accompanied by the appropriate songs. From this action in 1919 the Jingle dress spread throughout Chippewa/Ojibway territories.

"In the late 1920's the White Earth people gave the Jingle dress to the Fort Totten and the Sisseton Sioux, and from there it spread westward into Montana and the Dakotas.

"The Jingle dress maintained its popularity into the late 1940's and early 1950's. In the 1960's it was very rare to see a Jingle dress worn at a powwow. When someone did bring out her dress it was often considered a curiosity.

Jingling in Indian Country.

"Today, the Jingle dress has made a tremendous comeback thanks to those few proud Chippewa/Ojibway women who dared to continue to wear them and also to those powwow committees who recognized those few women and held contests for them at their powwows. In the late 1970's such contests were held in the eastern Dakotas and in Minnesota, and in a few years time, the interest in Jingle dresses had grown like never before. Even women from other tribes are beginning to make and wear them. The Jingle dress today is in great demand and is spreading in all directions." *

Upon close inspection one can see that the best Jingle dresses use cones made from the tops of Copenhagen chewing tobacco cans. When festooned in lines or chevron patterns, they touch against each other, making an attractive swishing and clacking sound.

In 1979 while at the Oil Celebration in Poplar, Montana, I once again saw the two girls from the Bay Area still wearing this same style of dress, only this time they were brighter in color. About three or four years ago many other young girls began to wear them, and now one sees them in increasing numbers. This year at the Red Bottom Powwow there are more than I have ever seen anywhere.

Because of the popularity of the Jingle dress style, we had been trying to get one for our daughter. She is losing interest in dancing, like most girls her age, and we hope it will rekindle her enthusiasm. We were finally able to purchase one from some Winnebago people from Minnesota. The dress has plain aluminum cones instead of the snoose can tops, but at $100 it is more affordable. Our girl will probably be one of the few Jingle dress dancers at our powwow in Cody as she spreads that innovative dress a bit further.

The precedent for such dresses is an old one. Some of the first dresses of the upper Missouri were made from mountain sheep skins, and the only decoration was a little remnant of tail in the center part of the yoke. Somewhere along the line, sewn-on decorations such as elk teeth, dentalia, cowrie shells, coins and

*History related by Florence Seaboy, White Earth Chippewa in United Tribes International Powwow Program, United Tribes Technical College, Bismarck, North Dakota.

other items began to be added around the yoke and even on the remainder of the dress. Eventually this style led to the Jingle dress and will no doubt continue to evolve, utilizing other creative sewn-on items.

The standard Jingle dress is more form-fitting, restricting the dancers in their side-to-side movements and forcing them to dance more vertically, up and down. They have no shawls and place their hands on hips like dancers did long ago. Some hold eagle feather fans and wear a plume on the backs of their heads. A Chippewa friend, Debbie Meyers, said the girls from other tribes who wear Jingle dresses do not dance correctly. Her mother told her that the proper step is similar to the Charleston.

The tin Copenhagen chewing tobacco tops can be purchased from U.S. Tobacco Company, 100 West Putnam Avenue, Greenwich, Connecticut, 06830. At this time $15 will buy 500 of them.

Another new phenomenon spreading like wild fire concerns the men's outfits. This is the "Grass Dance" attire that consists of colored cotton trousers and a separate shirt with long, brightly colored yarn fringes sewn on both pieces in chevron patterns. The unit is worn without bustles. A roach, ankle bells, Angora fetlocks, and moccasins complete the attire. It is quite attractive. The dancer moves from side to side, lifting his feet higher than the traditional dancer, and his shoulders sway to get the fringes to flow like the long prairie grass. It is much different from the other styles. The fancy dancers are more frantic; this style is more relaxed and smoother and flowing. Many of these dancers have two long antennae tipped with eagle plumes coming from the roach.

For many years I have seen at least one of these dancers at most powwows, but never more. Suddenly, within the last four or five years, more and more are apparent until they now have their own dance category and their own position in the Grand Entry. This is always a sure way to tell of their acceptance in the powwow.

I have yet to hear about the origin of this dance. It may be an updated, flamboyant version of an earlier conservative dance called the Northern Style Grass Dance. The older Northern Style favored black shirts and trousers decorated with shorter twisted

Men's Traditional Dancer. Owner: Mike Her Many Horses, Sioux, Wounded Knee, South Dakota.

Teenage Traditional Dancer. Owner: Rona Hugs, Crow, Crow Indian Reservation, Montana.

white fringe and may also have originated among the Chippewa. Shiney sequins applied in floral patterns mainly to the yoke, along with dangling feathers, formed the main decoration to the upper body. The headdress with antennaed plumes, and strings of larger beads, either looped around or hanging in front of the eyes, or a beaded rosette on the front of or on the side of the forehead, completed the upper portion. Large steel or brass bells tied above the Angora fetlocks were often worn, and many dancers were fond of wearing gauntlet gloves.

Most of the dancers of this type avoided using the traditional Crow belt bustle, according to Dave Hawley, a Gros Ventre from Ft. Belknap. Before this period, he says, the Crow belts or eagle feather bustles were considered religious, and this 1940's and 50's style may have been a movement toward a more secular, recreational activity. His brother Byard was such a dancer.

It is now called the Grass Dance, but the regular traditional dance of today has a long history of being called by the same name. Perhaps Grass Dance is an interim name. I have heard it called Yarn, Fringe, Frog, and Shake Dance, and I am sure other names will be used until a common term is accepted.

I look around and see that 80 to 90 percent of the Indian people are overweight, and that includes me as well. If the majority of the Indians are poverty stricken, then why are so many of us overweight? I think there are a number of reasons. One is because non-fattening food, such as fruits and vegetables, low-salt, low-fat items and lean meats, are more expensive. Second, frying is a traditional and preferred way to cook, but quite fattening. In addition, the Indian culture says that when you have visitors, whether at your home or at celebrations, you must feed them. Conversely, to be polite when offered food, you must eat. As a result, while attending a celebration or visiting people one is constantly eating. Recreation is more limited today than in the past, and excess calories are not burned off as in the days of old. Everyone has to eat, so there is a basic justification to indulge, and it is pleasurable. And because many people are overweight, there is no peer pressure to diet. All of these reasons combine to make us overweight. Once a child is exposed to these customs, he or she perpetuates them. My children will fry their food and feed their visitors; and good or bad, that is the way it will be.

A Blackfeet Indian elder. Photo: George P. Horse Capture.

Dancing in Sioux Country.

The Give-aways

After the Jingle Dance contest, pickups loaded with blankets and shawls begin to unload in front of the speaker's stand. This is a sign of a lengthy special, a give-away. The family sponsors come out in front of the speaker's stand and bring all of their give-away materials. They designate a moderator to narrate the activity and to extol the attributes of the person who is the focus of attention. He calls the name of a person in the audience who then comes up, accepts the gift and shakes hands with the sponsoring family.

Give-aways may be unique to the Indian people. A well-known example is the potlatch of the Northwest Coast Indians. Whenever a person or an event is worth remembering, it becomes a reason for this happening. After the extended family agrees to the event, for a year or longer they save proper materials, such as blankets, rugs, other Indian-related items, sheets, pillows and sometimes even a horse, as well as money. Then they schedule the program at their agreed-upon home reservation's powwow. Their moderator will explain the reason for the action which can range, for example, from a memorial for a deceased relative to the Indian naming of a relative, to the first time a relative dances Indian.

Instead of receiving a gift, the honored person and family give gifts to mark this ceremony. By giving gifts, the sponsors share their "wealth" with their friends and visitors. The gift establishes a tie and obligation between the giver and receiver and bonds everyone closer together. Give-aways happen at all powwows and are a vital part of our ways.

Since the 1950's a division had been growing between the college-educated Indian people and their traditions: each operated in their own areas which seldom joined. While attending a powwow at Lame Deer several years ago, I saw a change. I spent the afternoon watching give-aways. Here the Northern Cheyennes give entire tables of materials away. Toward late afternoon a family I knew announced their program and, lo and behold, the reason for their give-away was to honor their daughter, who had just won her college degree. I felt so happy for her and her proud family, but more so for the Indian people, because this action united the old with the new. We had successfully made the vital transition.

We walk around the outside of the arbor laughing, visiting, shaking hands with old friends and observing the age-old rite of girls giggling and flirting while the boys act macho and return their attentions.

During the specials, the dancers take off their roaches and put on fancy beaded baseball caps or take off other pieces of their outfits and just walk around and look on.

The emcee asks the audience to come early tomorrow because a rain dance is scheduled to help ease the drought, weather permitting.

After the give-aways we head back to the motel room in Wolf Point, take a brief shower, turn on the air conditioning full force, and settle down for an afternoon rest to conserve our strength for the evening. We wake later than expected and prepare for the evening Grand Entry at 7:00 p.m. There is hair combing and braiding, lipstick application, tying up moccasins and buckling down leggings, and the long awaited moment finally arrives when Daylight can at last try on her new Jingle dress for actual use. It fits nicely, and when she moves, it sounds like cut deer hooves. She walks back and forth across the room, bending over, picking things up, twisting, walking out into the hall and up and down the corridor, anything to hear that sound. She has finally achieved noise equality.

The Grand Entry

Somehow or other all of our dancers are ready. They're helped by my wife who devotes her energy to preparations, since she is unable to dance this time because of a sore foot. Speeding westward from Wolf Point, we arrive at Frazer just as the Grand Entry is starting. This is the most stately, spectacular and emotional part of powwow and makes all of the traveling worthwhile. This is the formal entry into the dance area and is a dedication and a recognition of the sponsors, the tribe, the public officials, and all the others. It is a time of pomp and circumstance.

The dance area is always defined. In my youth the powwow dancing, a secondary event at the end of the Sun Dance, took place in a large flat area not too far from the agency. Cut cottonwood limbs and other shrubbery anchored into the earth in a large circle designated the dance area. Dancing occupied a major portion of the space, with the spectators standing or sitting

Grand Entry.

on the very edge. The open-air arena was close to nature and in a natural setting.

As the popularity of powwows grew and spread to every viable Indian community, the committees became more concerned with weather conditions. About ten years ago reservation communities began to build I-beam roofed arbors. Such a structure negates the effects of inclement weather but also dulls the atmosphere; no natural light enters the dance area, so no grass grows, and with constant pounding feet, the soil floor becomes like concrete. When a small pebble inserts itself between a descending moccasin heel and the ground, the effect is quite startling.

Only a few reservations still maintain the older, open-air arbor. These include Rocky Boy, Cannonball, Rosebud, Blackfeet (they have astroturf), Northern Cheyenne, Ethete, and a few others. Although the heat and apprehension about weather is associated with the open air arbors, they do add life, color, and energy. I hope that not all of the reservations will convert to the dark I-beam arbor covers.

The arbors usually have the emcee's stand to the west and openings to the east and sometimes to the north and south as well. The main entrance is adjacent to the stand. It is through this entrance that the dancers enter for the Grand Entry. With minor variations, the categories and their positioning in the procession, which reflects their importance, are as follows. The flags are first. These include the American Flag; the Indian Flag, which is a buffalo fur-wrapped curved staff with eagle feathers; and usually another flag of some sort: this one could be Canadian, a state flag or a veteran flag. Indian communities place a high value on their warriors, so only veterans have the privilege of carrying these flags into the dance arena. They are adorned in their dance finery, their military uniforms, or a warbonnet. Abreast of each other, holding their flags on high, they lead the column.

Next in line may be distinguished individuals. This could include an important Indian person, Indian Princesses, or respected elders.

Each powwow committee designates a lead drum. This is the one that will work hand-in-hand with them with special tasks. It is this honored drum that will sing the Grand Entry song, either

by singing the same song several times until all the dancers have entered, or by maintaining the rhythm of the drum after their song ends, while a subsequent drum picks up the rhythm and sings another appropriate song, thus sharing the musical load. This latter system occasionally works well, but when there is a break in the tempo between drums, the happy mood of the Grand Entry is broken.

A mobile refreshment stand.

The first dancers to enter the arena in the Grand Entry are the male traditionals. Long ago this dance was called the Crow Belt, and has evolved into the Grass Dance. But with the advent of the new "Yarn" dancers, the term "Grass Dance" now refers to them while "Traditional" describes the older type. Two things designate a traditional dancer: outfit and age. The outfit's most

Girl's Traditional Dancer. Owner: Elizabeth Starr Horse Capture, Gros Ventre, Ft. Belknap Indian Reservation, Montana.

Women's Traditional Dancer. Owner: Lawanda Little Coyote, Northern **Cheyenne**, Northern Cheyenne Indian Reservation, Montana.

distinguishing characteristic is the style of bustle. Different styles designate different types of dancers. The traditionalist wears black-tipped golden eagle feathers in a distinctive manner.

It is said that the initial traditional Grass Dance outfit came from the Heluska society of the Omaha tribe and slowly spread northward, some of the integral paraphernalia changing as the style moved from tribe to tribe. A Lakota friend and dancer from Wounded Knee, Mike Her Many Horses, states that his grandfather Ben Marrowbone said that in the mid-1870's a woman from Spotted Tail's band of Rosebud Sioux married a Omaha man and the Omaha people gave this dance to them as a wedding gift. Since then, there has been peace between the two tribes. From the Sioux it traveled to the Assiniboine, from the Assiniboine to the Gros Ventre, then to the Blackfeet and beyond. The most distinctive item was probably the bustle from which the name arose. At one time it may have been made of braided grass, or perhaps its feathers moved like the grass. This piece, called the Crow belt, is a rigid affair with two cloth trailers bedecked with eagle feathers. Today there are only a few Crow belts in use, with most present-day dancers wearing some sort of butterfly-hinged bustles with the feathers becoming more and more extended.

Dr. Chuck Ross, Lakota educator and author, believes that long ago Crow belts were sacred and that his people could dance at the gatherings, but only those holding special offices could wear the feathered bustles. Later, as the traditional lifestyle changed with the disappearance of the buffalo and the rise of reservations, great changes also came to this aspect of the native culture. For many reasons, a number of Indian people signed up with western shows in the latter half of the 1800's, particularly Buffalo Bill's Wild West show. Because of the ordeals and trauma they were undergoing at home, they may have been seeking solace in a medium that seemed to delay the death of their preferred lifestyle.

It seems reasonable to assume that the costumes of actors in the show would have been various objects from their traditional wardrobe. To add more spice and theatrics, they wore parts of the Crow belt dance attire, such as the headdress, armbands, and even the feathered bustles. With the waning of the traditions and the actors' need to make money as flashing performers, the objects lost their sacredness and were used indiscriminately by all. The religious aspect of the belt was destroyed. This "commercial" adjustment spread along the pipeline north and west, reaching Montana by the first decade of the twentieth century; and it affected many other aspects of Indian culture as well, according to Ross.

One can speculate that perhaps some dancers, not traditionally entitled to wear the bustle, continued to do without them. Eventually this secular practice may have evolved into the Northern Plains Grass Dance style of the 1940's, then into that of the Grass or Yarn dancers of today.

This category of dance has the closest link with the past. Painted leggings, mirror boards, eagle-wing fans, hairpipe breast plates, otterskin breast plates, pouches, knife cases, shields, and hoops are presented by these dancers. By closely watching and appreciating these classic dancers, one can see the warriors of old on their way to a war path or birds of the prairie during mating season.

The other element of a traditional dancer is age. This stately, classical dance style features distinguished gestures and does not require as much exertion as other dances; therefore, it is more suitable for the older gentlemen. However, because of its relationship to the past, many young people prefer it to flashier, recent dances; so these dancers dance in the traditional style and category.

Next in line are the men fancy dancers. The contemporary expression of this category has undergone complex evolutions, spinning off from the original Grass Dance or Northern Style Grass Dance. It opens new frontiers by utilizing brightly colored chicken hackle feathers instead of eagle feathers. The shoulder bustles, in addition to the regular ones, also have evolved. These U-shaped bustles are highly flexible and swing and twist with the dancers' movements. With the addition of the purple, red, yellow, green, and other brightly colored feathers incorporated into the sets of bustles, these dancers not only flutter, but are energetic and frantic.

Next in line are the women traditionals. Like the men, the women in this category have a closer relationship with the ancient traditions which allows them to wear buckskin dresses,

At the wallowing hole.

elk teeth, wool, cowrie, dentalium, and other old decorations. With the addition of a purse, perhaps a fan, a feather in the hair, as well as high-topped moccasins, these ladies, with graceful dignity and classical up and down dance movements, enter the arena in single file and add much class to the proceedings.

The girl's Shawl or Fancy Dance group are next. To me, they are the most beautiful of all. Young girls have a consuming propensity to dance, more so than their male counterparts. Here that ability can be fully realized. In addition to their youthful charm, these young girls' outfits, with some assistance from their families, are the most creative in the powwow circuit. Their yokes allow them great creative versatility. These can be under or over the shawl, and their dresses can be a multitude of hairpipes, beads, sequins, ribbons and all the rest. They can have French braids, two braids, no braids, and an endless variety of feather tie styles.

Perhaps the greatest area for creativity is their shawls. Spread across the back, the shawl is held by the ends. As the dancers take flight, these shawl wings help them to soar and twist in the clouds, only rarely touching the earth. It is here that the dancers declare their allegiance to a reservation, a club, a symbol, a color, a design, an animal, a totem, or an abstract. The decoration could be appliqued cloth, embroidery, bead, silkscreen, paint, sequins, and things you have never heard of before. It is mesmerizing to see all these young girls dancing the same dance, but no two doing it alike. All are clothed in great creations of beauty and possess an energy that is evinced in their gymnastics and attire.

After the girl's Shawl or Fancy division, the new category of Jingle Dresses emerges as the Grass Dancers sometimes follow the men's Fancy or sometimes they are intermixed. However, the younger category follows the older groups. The "tiny tots" enter last and are miniature versions of the adult categories. This entire entry process takes from 20-45 minutes and is quite moving.

When I am an active part of the Grand Entry, I feel good, with my bustle feathers fluttering in the breeze and my headdress centered and firmly attached. I wait in line, slowly walking toward the entrance among all the others watching the Grand Entry in front take place. As I approach, the rhythm of the drum becomes stronger, and I mentally mark a spot on the ground where I will start dancing. At that spot my body leans forward, tensing, and my descending moccasin sets the bells ringing, my knee comes up higher, and then I am in the arena, dancing in rhythm with all the others, "shaking the earth."

I feel good knowing that with the investment of all the time and expense involved, I am finally here. As I adjust the space between the people in front and in back of me, I am part of the widening circle of dancers, each a living part of the tradition that is Indian. As the perspiration begins, I dance my best, continuing to enter clockwise in ever-tightening circles. The honor guard breaks off and stands abreast, facing the speaker's stand. Soon, the chemistry, the ambience, and the magic are just right. While vigorously dancing, an irrefutable awareness arises that I am close to the center, to the essence of life. As the world dissolves in color and music around me, a warm spiritual feeling spreads throughout the heart and body, and the song and dance carry me away from the heat and earth. Another zone of awareness, a detachment, is entered: My feet, body, and arms move automatically to the rhythm of life. My fellow dancers are a part of me and I a part of them. I realize that life could not get much better than this moment and it is a gift from the creator. As the countless eagle feathers flutter before my eyes, I realize that this is Indian – this is powwow.

Eventually the song ends and the moment passes, but it will be back; it always is. This is what makes our lives rich and unique.

As traditional dancers run out of internal space, they dance in place, facing the center until the song ends. Although the Grand Entry is perhaps the most exciting activity in the powwow, the immediate period afterwards is perhaps the most tedious. Once a dancer has performed his best and is hot, his perspiration and adrenalin flowing, he must stop for formalities. Now they sing two songs. The first is a flag song and is patriotic in nature. The dancers all stand silently. The next song is an honor song, perhaps honoring the whole gathering. Everyone dances in place with bells ringing. These songs are usually sung by the same drum.

When the two songs are complete, the emceee introduces a respected elder from the community who gives the benediction.

Young Girl's Traditional Dancer. Owner: Gail Wallowing Bull, Arapaho/Northern Cheyenne, Lame Deer, Montana.

Young Boy's Fancy Dancer. Owner: Sean Chandler, Gros Ventre, Billings, Montana.

This prayer is usually rendered in a native language which most of the participants do not understand because they are from elsewhere. It matters little, because we know that this is a prayer, and as such, a mood of spirituality spreads throughout the arena. We all say our little special prayer, hoping that we have a good time, that we will meet relatives and friends, and that we will have a safe journey home. It is a good feeling. When the elder finishes, there is no applause.

Next the emcee introduces a politician or some other speaker. If it is a politician, he usually speaks too long, and the mind wanders as the feet begin to tire. This time, however, it is the local princess who welcomes everyone. Most of the time we cannot hear her, because she either does not speak directly into the microphone or the sound system is malfunctioning again. This happens at most powwows and is almost expected, albeit annoying. We smile at her and feel good, because we know she is doing a good job and that she feels good, too. This may be her moment and we wish her well. When she finishes, we all shake our leg bells or clap and relax, for this usually marks the end of the formal session.

The Princess

Royalty means "Princess(es)." These are the young ladies chosen in some fashion from their respective community powwows to bear the title of Princess, Princess Runner-up, Princess Attendants, etc. They wear beaded crowns and cloth banners that proclaim their titles. The Indian race, however, does not believe in the European concept of royalty; and a leader is recognized for demonstrated ability rather

A pair of princesses. On the left is Miss Plains Indian Museum, 1987, Kaylene Shane, a Crow, of Crow Indian Reservation, Montana. She was succeeded by Elizabeth Olney, a Chippewa/Cree of Rocky Boy Indian Reservation, Montana, who was Miss Plains Indian Museum, 1988, and is pictured on the right.

Miss Plains Indian Museum 1988, Elizabeth Olney (left) and Miss Plains Indian Museum 1987 (right) joined by their families and friends.

than for "blue blood." The concept of royalty was first introduced by immigrants, who brought European beliefs with them and gained favor calling the daughters of Indian leaders "princesses." But this name was as valid as the derogatory terms "bucks" for men and "squaws" for women. Even to this day, innumerable white people claim an Indian grandmother, usually a Cherokee and usually a princess. In the contemporary period, the term probably gained popularity in Oklahoma and spread from there.

Although some outside organizations and individuals frown upon Princess contests, from an internal view, they are an accepted form of achievement. Here the young ladies can engage in good natured rivalry and be goal-oriented. This allows them some format for developing their poise, communication ability and an outlet to the outer world. Most Indian communities have some form of this "royalty," leading up to the season finale, the choosing of Miss Indian America at United Tribes Technical College in Bismarck during the second weekend in September.

After the formalities are completed, the emcee calls for the next drum to sing an inter-tribal. This means that the next drum will sing a song that is classified as a Grass Dance or a war dance, and everyone can dance to it. Many people come just to dance inter-tribals, and they never compete in the contests or the other specials. This is recreation time. This is why we travel many hundreds of miles: to inter-tribal with all of our people and friends. It is very wonderful.

After this rigorous dance, the emcee asks the audience, "How would you guys like to do that in your aerobics group?"

When walking back to my seat, I wish I had brought the folding chair from the van, so that I could rest on it without crushing my tail feathers. And a cold Diet Coke would really be good about now.

The Inter-tribals

Because I enjoy dancing so much, one time I tried to remember why I had not danced all my life, instead of only as an adult. Thinking back to my childhood, when I was raised by my grandmother, I remembered that she had two houses. One was a log house that was the center of activity, and the other was a frame house used for different purposes. At the time of this memory a male relative was living there by the name of Felix Frog – we kids called him Felix the Frog. He was not an elder, as I remember, but he had strong traditions. One winter's day he had a pot on top of the potbellied stove and was cooking something different, because it bubbled there all day. For some reason a couple of us kids visited him, and he started to sing Indian. He sang some Grass Dance songs, and they must have been pretty special, because soon we were dancing around the pot and the stove, making all the fancy body moves and enjoying it greatly. I do not ever remember dancing before, but we had seen others do it, and we knew we could do it just as well or better. After he finished singing, I remember he took the pot off the stove and removed the cover. Inside was a beaver tail. This was the first time I had ever seen beaver tail soup. I do not remember if I ate the soup or not, but I hope so. This is the first time I remember dancing, but this memory still does not satisfy my bewilderment about why I did not dance more.

Inter-tribals are always good for me. As the dance begins we are all still sweaty and the song is generally a good one. After all the days in the city, music again permeates our souls and makes us all energetic and lively. As I dance, a special sense develops, and I feel like a warrior in days of old going to battle. Beside me and in front and in back are my people. We are all going to the same place and we are all happy and sharing a grand adventure. We rejoice in dancing in the style of our grandfathers; and as the sense increases, one feels stronger, bends over farther, the feet lift higher and the bells ring clearer.

While concentrating on getting the steps right with the drum beat and holding your arms half bent, twisting your body in certain ways and lifting your head up in a cocky sort of way, you often catch a friend's eye. You both dance towards each other, never missing a beat, and smiling, you shake hands out on the dance floor and maybe shout something like, "It's good to see you" or "You're looking good." Then each dances off in a different direction, hoping to meet again later to visit. Rejoining the floor, you are all in rhythm, all with friends.

On Being Indian

Being an Indian in this world is not easy. If you are a laborer or

Men's Traditional Dancer. Owner: Al Chandler, Gros Ventre, Billings, Montana.

Girl's Jingle Dress Dancer. Owner: Daylight Horse Capture, Gros Ventre, Cody, Wyoming.

an unskilled worker, you are usually ridiculed at work by the surrounding rednecks. People inquire if you can do a rain dance because it is dry, or ask where is your squaw (meaning your wife), or do you have papooses (meaning babies). This happens all the time. Meeting racism on every front changes you, perhaps distorts you. Reality takes on a different hue and one cannot relax. When your children come home from the city school and tell you some white kid called them prairie niggers, you realize that the cycle of racism is still alive and thriving in Indian country. Whether the racist comments are said as a joke or hatefully, the effect is the same. It is destructive to all parties, and never ceases. The only place to really relax is back home on the reservation surrounded by your people.

As he does everywhere, the Great Spirit in his infinite wisdom bestows a balance here, too. So, if there is a bad part, there is also a good part. It's good being Indian. As we drive across the country and see the trees and coulees and the sage brush and grass covering the prairie, we know this is Indian country, and long ago buffalo covered it from horizon to horizon. We know this has always been our land. We will never emigrate to the British Isles or to Australia or to anywhere. This is our home, good or bad. It is our home and we stick with it, because this is the earth. This is our earth and these hills are our hills. It doesn't matter who owns the deed to the land, because these paper holders change and they will always change. But these hills and mountains and valleys and coulees and bluffs are ours, the Indian people's. They have always been ours and they always will be. We know this. It makes us feel good. No one can change this, and it does not matter if we are poor or not.

They say that no matter where an Indian dies, he always comes home. In my family this is true. My uncle died in California and the family brought him home. This has happened with many other families. Somehow it does not seem right to be buried far away. You have got to be surrounded by your people even then. This is another benefit of being Indian. We know where we came from and we know where we are going to be buried. We have a center to our lives. Out of all this chaos, there is a certain order. We're the only ones in this country who have that advantage. That is good for us.

A young winner.

Proud Traditional dancers.

A grass dancer. Photo: Devendra Shrikhande.

The Specials

Although most tribes of the Northern Plains share general traits, each has developed special views, activities, and ceremonies. On occasion the powwow committee will recreate a community-oriented dance from the 1930's or 40's when values were different and communities more united. It is from this era that one can see the Owl Dance, very seldom performed nowadays and consisting of a slower dance where a man and a woman hold each other, much like a waltz. It is more intimate and special. Only dances based on competition are active and thriving today; many more types should be revived.

About three or four years ago we were fortunate enough to take part in such a revival. It, of course, happened at the Red Bottom Celebration in Fraser and as the calendar would have it, on Father's Day.

The emcee's booming voice announced that they were having a special dance for fathers and would all the fathers please get out into the arbor. This included all fathers, both traditionally attired and those in civilian clothes. The floor became crowded as fathers lined up in single file in a large circle and began to do a sort of round dance in a clockwise direction to an appropriate song.

After completing one turn around the arbor, the emcee's voice called each child to come and hold his father's hand and dance with him. Quickly the arbor became filled with children of all sizes as they scampered towards their fathers. As the drum and song continued, we all danced together.

After completing another circle of the arbor, the dancers heard the emcee once again, saying, "All right, you wives, it's your turn." The women came in from the outside, stepping between the dancers to form an inner adjacent ring of dancers that went counterclockwise against the clockwise movement of the men. With the men facing in and the women facing out, there was eye-to-eye contact between them as they danced and met one another. Upon meeting, the women would smile at the men, shake their hands and wish them happy Father's Day. The dance was quite emotional and joyous. Upon its conclusion we all knew we had taken part in something very special.

Girl's Fancy Dancer. Owner: Arlena Thompson, Navajo, Chinle, Arizona.

Girl's Tiny Tot Traditional Dancer. Owner: Putt Thompson, adopted by Crow Indians, Crow Indian Reservation, Montana.

Arbor spectators.

Steve Spider, a champion traditional dancer.

The Sport

As a person over 50, and I hope occasionally dignified, I prefer the traditional dance. In the long haul it preserves tradition and is the foundation of the whole powwow structure. Frequently I admire the intensity, dexterity and fierceness of the younger dancers, as their bodies twist and gyrate and perspiration shines on their faces. Determination is there, but also great joy. The dances of the powwow are an important competitive medium for our young people, as well as being a "sport" and a way of showing their capabilities and athletic talents.

Long ago, during the Buffalo days, the energetic young men went off to war to demonstrate their prowess and abilities. Returning home, they gained honor and recognition for their capabilities and achieved status and a place in their world. Today, because of the parochial and isolated lifestyles of the Indian people, a professional Indian baseball player, basketball player, violin player, or any other similar professional is very rare. We don't have the economic base to train our youngsters in these fields, nor do we have the followup support from within our group to continue such a course. In our world there are two fundamental areas where one can compete to earn honor and prestige. One is the rodeo; the other is the powwow.

The powwow's participants form a distinct sub-group, and many attend twenty or more powwows annually. They must know the songs to become good dancers, because any mistake, such as an extra step, may disqualify them from competition. The outstanding money dancers gain far-flung reputations for their skills, and sponsoring organizations are always pleased to have them attend. Many dancers participate with a fervor that can be compared to that of the warriors and their battles of long ago. Many are quite successful and tour the country to compete with each other. They gain reputations, and the physical expenditure is perhaps even more strenuous than in the early days, although it is never fatal. In powwow you can do all these things and at the same time maintain a tradition.

Often, my family, along with several hundred other families, rendezvous at predetermined powwows across the plains. These include Rocky Boy, Fort Belknap, the Oil Celebration, Fort Kipp and others. Because powwows must occur on vast acreages of undeveloped land, facilities are limited and usually consist only of outhouses and water. Nonetheless, the family gathers, pitching small camping tents of various sizes and colors or sleeping in the backs of their camper pickups. There is always a fire going, either on the ground or in the Coleman, and coffee brewing. Unfolding their chairs, the family, which includes grandparents, parents, children and grandchildren, close cousins, and more distant relatives, sit around drinking coffee and visiting while the kids play in the dirt. In this manner, we all become reacquainted and find out what happened to so and so, who divorced whom, who is going to college and who is still bumming around. In spite of the oppressive heat, infernal insects, and the pervasive dust, the gathering and visiting continue unabated. Our cousin Kathleen recently observed, "Who else but Indians would drive hundreds of miles, sit on sweltering prairie for days, sleep on the hard ground, and endure other hardships too numerous to mention, just to visit?" All powwowers do; that's their job.

The Rodeo

Some people consider a powwow a total celebration only when it is accompanied by an Indian rodeo. Although the two activities seem completely different, they in fact share a number of traits. The basic structure and terminology is similar. At a rodeo there is a speaker's stand, the same as at a powwow. When the horsemen enter the arena, like the dancers, they circle until everyone is in, and the flag bearers stand in front of the stand. This action is called a Grand Entry in both events. Almost all of the contestants are numbered for the competition. Of course, rodeos do not have "inter-tribals" where anyone can come in and participate, but all the other elements are the same. And, of course, both are of the West. So, Cowboys and Indians are not so different and remember, Indians were "cowboys" before anyone else. Usually the two events happen at the same time, but rarely does one participant compete in both; there seem to be rodeo Indians and powwow Indians, with the two never seriously meeting. I am pleased that Red Bottom does not have a rodeo.

Young Boy's Traditional Dancer. Owner: Jeff Wallowing Bull, Arapaho/Northern Cheyenne, Lame Deer, Montana.

Men's Traditional "Crow" Dancer. Owner: Putt Thompson, adopted by Crow Indians, Crow Indian Reservation, Montana.

The Judging

Jerry Fiddler, a Lakota friend from Eagle Butte and a champion traditional dancer, says he believes that one reason for drastic changes in attire, fads, and the dancing structure itself, is due to judging. All through the year, the powwow committee struggles with complex fund-raising, difficult scheduling, fancy arrangements with concessioners; and they do it all reasonably well. Yet the selection of judges is done on an *ad hoc* basis. Frequently people who have never danced themselves end up judging the dancers. Being relatively inexperienced, they go for flash rather than style. Some contest dancers notice who wins, analyze that person's style and/or outfit and emulate the winners because they know that the presentation was effective. Therefore, rapid deviation from the standard may occur. Several remedies are possible, and the major one is already taking place at some Sioux powwows. The powwow committee tells the emcee to stress traditional values and styles throughout the powwow. This applies to the singers who will be urged to sing the very old songs, and the value is then passed on to the dancers who must dance to them. This type of regimen is tough for some dancers and singers, but in the long run, may prove very effective in maintaining culture.

To Fiddler, it seems reasonable to assume that someone who is conscientious, unbiased and fair could be designated dance judge, and this should be the goal of the dance committee. These judges would be similar to the officials at basketball, baseball and football games. In those sports, umpires or judges aren't chosen from the stands. This system may work or it may not. Much of the responsibility falls, of course, upon the judge, who must be well-versed in tradition if that is what direction is desired. It's worth a shot, Fiddler says.

Sometime a little after 9:00 p.m., while the body still tingles and everybody has spunk and energy, the inter-tribal dance is ended with an announcement of an upcoming give-away special. Give-aways are unique to each Indian community, but I don't think that any of them should be done in the evening, but in their own special time, the afternoon. Evenings are for dancing. Anyway, when cars and pickups begin unloading material, you know a give-away is coming up. We decide to wrap it up and go home the next day. After our showers we settle comfortably in bed in the air-conditioned room, and we experience a warm glow because of everything we have seen and done that day. It was a good one.

The 49

The younger generation has its own unique activity that takes place after the regular dancing finishes, usually well after midnight. They gather at a predetermined and remote site on the prairie to do a "49." One well-known explanation of this name states that as fifty Oklahoma Indian soldiers went off to battle in one of the World Wars, they vowed to get together upon their return to celebrate by dancing and singing. A song was to be sung for each warrior. When the time finally arrived, they sang only 49 songs, because one soldier never returned.

The dance scene is quite dark and the young adults are celebrating. Arms around each other's shoulders, the "leader" starts a song and the others join in as they dance a round-dance step. Gopher holes, rocks and cactus notwithstanding, the frivolity often continues until dawn.

The songs for most part use English words, but are performed as in the regular song structure. Two examples of the English words in the romantic verses are as follows:

> Oh yes, I love you, honey dear,
> I don't care if you've been married 15 times,
> I'll get you yet!
>
> Honey, love me, hug me, hold me close
> to you, sweetheart
> Because you're my one and only
> I still love you.

Such a dance is an accepted part of a celebration, and allows the youngsters their own "hop." The following morning is quieter than usual with the absence of the "49ers." When they finally appear in the afternoon, many carry a "49" mark.

Chico Her Many Horses, winner of the Eb Tarr Special Gun Award at Cody, Wyoming.

Heading Home

My inner alarm clock goes off at 7:00 a.m., and I start rustling around. Slowly the others follow suit, and we are at breakfast an hour later. We head for the powwow grounds after dressing and stop to see who won the Jingle dress raffle. It was not us, but the stop gives us the chance to say goodbye until next year. Then we head toward home.

Having a little time, we take a roundabout route that goes through Fort Belknap – my reservation. It is very beautiful. Adjacent to the James Kipp Bridge where it crosses the Missouri River, near the Charlie Russell Game Refuge, we see a prairie fire. We had seen its smoke hours before. It looks like it is burning five miles long. It's a pity when such fires kill animals or burn property, but I think it bestows a certain cleansing process to the trees and grass. After the fire passes and the rain comes, an entire new growth flourishes and renews everything. It is an ancient cycle.

We are on our last leg, and the weather is cooling off. It was so hot earlier that I had turned on the air conditioning and had to watch the heat gauge, because we had been boiling over. Something in the radiator wasn't functioning correctly, but now the coolness in the air is a pure pleasure.

The sun is about 20 degrees up from the west. It is setting and casts a certain light that makes everything mellow yet brilliant. This is a time for photographers and those who appreciate Mother Nature's beauty.

When returning from a powwow you always experience a certain let-down, a kind of post-depression you get after any exciting event. There is a melancholy feeling because you realize you won't see that combination of special friends and relatives together ever again. You know it was a special time attended by special people and now everyone has gone his separate way.

We always leave early because we have a tremendous distance to travel, and we want to get home before dark to get a little rest. Because tomorrow, rain or shine, we go back to work. But if the One Above smiles on us, there will be endless powwows.

Rosebud riders.

Women's Traditional Dancer. Owner: Gloria Goggles, Sioux, Ethete, Wyoming.

Boy's Tiny Tot Traditional Dancer. Owner: Tabor White Buffalo, Sioux, Ethete, Wyoming.

NORTHERN PLAINS INDIAN RESERVATIONS

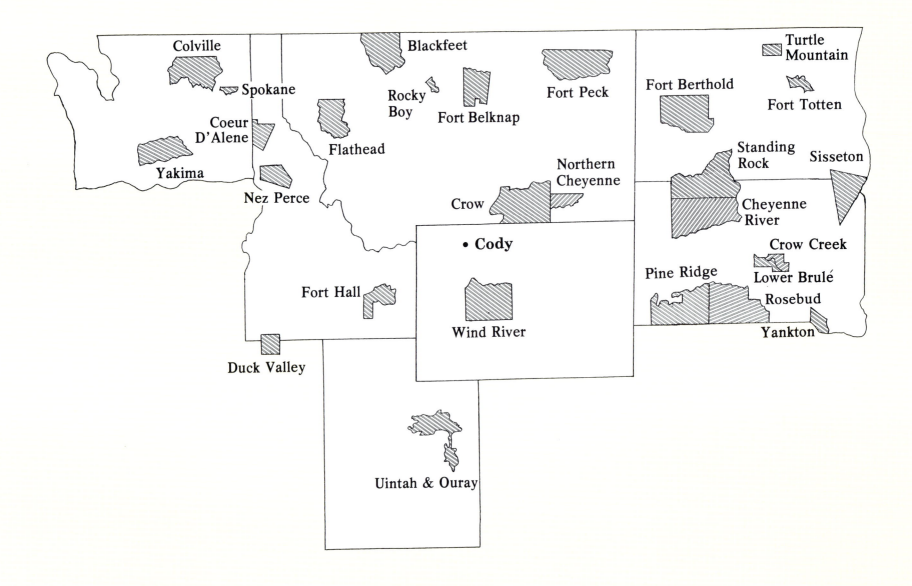

POWWOWS OF INTEREST

Idaho

Coeur d'Alene Annual Powwow (Coeur d'Alene), Worley, last weekend in July. Call tribal office at 208-274-3101 for information.

Shoshone-Paiute Annual 4th of July Powwow (Duck Valley Indian Reservation), Owyhee, first week in July. Call tribal office at 702-757-3161 for information.

Shoshone-Bannock Indian Festival and Rodeo (Fort Hall Indian Reservation), Fort Hall, second week in August. Call tribal office at 208-238-3700 for information.

Chief Joseph and Warriors Powwow Memorial for Chief Joseph (Nez Perce Indian Reservation), Lapwai, third weekend in June. Call tribal office at 208-843-2253 for information.

Montana

North American Indian Days (Blackfeet Indian Reservation), Browning, second weekend in July. Call tribal office at 406-338-7522 for information.

Crow Fair (Crow Indian Reservation), Crow Agency, third weekend in August. Call tribal office at 406-638-2601 for information.

Arlee Annual Powwow, (Flathead Indian Reservation), Arlee, first week in July. Call tribal office at 406-745-4242 for information.

Milk River Indian Days (Fort Belknap Indian Reservation), Fort Belknap Agency, last weekend in July. Call tribal office at 406-353-2205 for information.

Red Bottom Celebration (Fort Peck Indian Reservation), Fraser, third weekend in June. Call tribal office at 406-768-5155 for information.

Fourth of July Annual Powwow (Northern Cheyenne Indian Reservation), Lame Deer, first week in July. Call tribal office at 406-477-6284 for information.

Rocky Boy Annual Powwow (Rocky Boy Indian Reservation), Rocky Boy Agency, first weekend in August. Call tribal office at 406-395-4291 for information.

North Dakota

Little Shell Powwow (Fort Berthold Indian Reservation), New Town, second weekend in August. Call tribal office at 701-627-4781 for information.

Fort Totten Annual Wacipi, (Fort Totten Indian Reservation), Fort Totten, last weekend in July. Call tribal office at 701-766-4221 for information.

Turtle Mountain Annual Labor Day Powwow, (Turtle Mountain Indian Reservation), Belcourt, Labor Day Weekend. Call tribal office at 701-477-6451 for information.

South Dakota

Cheyenne River Labor Day Powwow (Cheyenne River Indian Reservation), Eagle Butte, Labor Day Weekend. Call tribal office at 605-964-4155 for information.

Annual Crow Creek Powwow (Crow Creek Indian Reservation), Pierre, third weekend in August. Call tribal office at 605-245-2221 for information.

Lower Brule Annual Powwow (Lower Brule Indian Reservation), Lower Brule, second weekend in August. Call tribal office at 605-473-5316 for information.

Rosebud Annual Powwow and Fair (Rosebud Indian Reservation), Rosebud, third weekend in August. Call tribal office at 605-747-2381 for information.

Sisseton Wahpeton Powwow (Sisseton Indian Reservation), Sisseton, first week in July. Call tribal office at 605-698-7676 for information.

Standing Rock Annual Powwow (Standing Rock Indian Reservation), Fort Yates, first week in August. Call tribal office at 701-854-3431 for information.

Fort Randall Annual Powwow (Yankton Indian Reservation), Lake Andes, first weekend in August. Call tribal office at 605-384-3804 for information.

Utah

Northern Ute Annual Powwow and Rodeo (Uintah and Ouray Indian Reservation), Fort Duchesne, first week in July. Call tribal office at 801-722-5141 for information.

Washington

Drum and Feather Club's Annual Fourth of July Powwow (Colville Indian Reservation), Colville Indian Agency, first week in July. Call tribal office at 509-634-4711 for information.

Spokane Indians Labor Day Powwow (Spokane Indian Reservation), Wellpinit, Labor Day Weekend. Call tribal office at 509-258-4581 for information.

Fourth of July Powwow (Yakima Indian Reservation), White Swan, first week in July. Call tribal office at 509-865-5121 for information.

Wyoming

Shoshone Indian Days (Wind River Indian Reservation), Fort Washakie, third weekend in June. Call tribal office at 307-255-8265 for information.

Plains Indian Museum Annual Powwow (Buffalo Bill Historical Center), Cody, last weekend in June. Call Buffalo Bill Historical Center at 307-587-4771 for information.

Ethete Powwow (Wind River Indian Reservation), Ethete, third weekend in July. Call tribal office at 307-255-8265 for information.

LENDERS TO THE EXHIBITION

December Ariwite, Shoshone-Bannock, Ft. Hall, Idaho: Girl's Traditional Dancer Outfit.

Oriann Baker, Chippewa, Sisseton Indian Reservation, South Dakota: Women's Fancy Dancer Outfit.

Audrey Belgarde, Chippewa, Billings, Montana: Girl's Tiny Tot Jingle Dress Dancer Outfit.

Buffalo Chips, Billings, Montana/Cody, Wyoming: Materials for Contemporary Crafts, Contemporary Jewelery.

Orbana Cady, Shoshone, Dubois, Wyoming: Shawls.

Mr. and Mrs. Al Chandler, Billings, Montana: Three Quilts, Shawl, Men's Traditional Dancer Outfit.

Dawn Chandler, Gros Ventre, Beaverton, Oregon: Young Girl's Traditional Dancer Outfit.

Sean Chandler, Gros Ventre, Billings, Montana: Young Boy's Fancy Dancer Outfit.

Danna Clark-Runs Above, Assiniboine, Ft. Peck Indian Reservation, Montana: Women's Jingle Dress Dancer Outfit.

Elijah Cobb, New York, New York: Color Photographs.

Mr. and Mrs. J. Day, Sioux/Assiniboine, Ft. Peck Indian Reservation, Montana: Four Shawls, Women's Traditional Dancer Outfit, Traditional "Chief" Dancer Outfit.

Jay Fox, Northern Cheyenne, Busby, Montana: Grass Dancer Outfit.

Loren Fredericks, Mandan, North Dakota: Quilt.

Gloria Goggles, Sioux, Ethete, Wyoming: Two Women's Traditional Dancer Outfits.

Mike Her Many Horses, Sioux, Wounded Knee, South Dakota: Men's Traditional Dancer Outfit.

Daylight Horse Capture, Gros Ventre, Cody, Wyoming: Girl's Jingle Dress Dancer Outfit.

Elizabeth Starr Horse Capture, Gros Ventre, Ft. Belknap Indian Reservation, Montana: Girl's Traditional Dancer Outfit.

George P. Horse Capture, Gros Ventre, Cody, Wyoming: Traditional "Chief" Dancer Outfit.

George P. Horse Capture, Jr., Gros Ventre, Hays, Montana: Baby Carrier.

Joseph D. Horse Capture, Gros Ventre, Cody, Wyoming: Young Boy's Fancy Dancer Outfit.

Kay-Karol Horse Capture, Cody, Wyoming: Barrettes, Dress, Slips, Shawl.

Rona Hugs, Crow, Crow Indian Reservation, Montana: Teenage Traditional Dancer Outfit.

JR's Fashions for Men, Cody, Wyoming: Pendleton Blankets.

Denise Lajimodiere, Belcourt, North Dakota: Women's Jingle Dress Dancer Outfit.

Brent Lee, Cody, Wyoming: United States Navy Uniform.

Lawanda Little Coyote, Northern Cheyenne, Northern Cheyenne Indian Reservation, Montana: Women's Traditional Dancer Outfit.

Lee Lone Bear, Northern Cheyenne, Lame Deer, Montana: Granddaughter's Tiny Tot Traditional Dancer Outfit.

Missouri Breaks Industries, Timber Lake, South Dakota: Quilted Baby Carrier.

Myrtle Old Man, Arapaho, Arapahoe, Wyoming: Young Girl's Jingle Dress Dancer Outfit.

Gary Real Bird, Crow, Crow Indian Reservation, Montana: Chief's Outfit.

Margaret Ross, Mandan/Hidatsa, Garrison, North Dakota: Girl's Fancy Dancer Outfit.

Linda Saroni, Cody, Wyoming: Blouse.

Kaylene Shane, Crow, Crow Indian Reservation, Montana: Princess Outfit.

Sioux Trading Post, Rapid City, South Dakota: Belt Buckles.

Delores Thayer, Shoshone, Fort Washakie, Wyoming: Shawls.

Arlena Thompson, Navajo, Chinle, Arizona: Girl's Fancy Dancer Outfit.

Putt Thompson, adopted by Crow Indians, Custer Battlefield, Montana: Men's Traditional "Crow" Dancer Outfit, Girl's Tiny Tot Traditional Dancer Outfit.

Jeff Wallowing Bull, Arapaho/Northern Cheyenne, Lame Deer, Montana: Young Boy's Traditional Dancer Outfit.

Gail Wallowing Bull, Arapaho/Northern Cheyenne, Lame Deer, Montana: Young Girl's Traditional Dancer Outfit.

Western Trading Post, Denver, Colorado: Beaded Sneakers.

Tabor White Buffalo, Sioux, Ethete, Wyoming: Boy's Tiny Tot Traditional Dancer Outfit.

Carla White Grass, Blackfeet, Browning, Montana: Men's Grass Dancer Outfit.

Girl's Traditional Dancer. Owner: December Ariwite, Shoshone-Bannock, Ft. Hall, Idaho.

Traditional "Chief" Dancer. Owner: Joe Day, Sioux/Assiniboine, Ft. Peck Indian Reservation, Montana.

Fifteen minutes until Grand Entry.

Dressing for the journey home.

Boy's Fancy Dancer. Owner: Joseph D. Horse Capture, Gros Ventre, Cody, Wyoming.

Chief's Outfit. Owner: Gary Real Bird, Crow, Crow Indian Reservation, Montana.

Twilight during summer powwow.